Coming Full Circle

*A Unique Collection of
Inspirational Poetry,
Proverbs and
Spiritual Affirmations*

by

Sy'needa Penland

Copyright © 2016 by Sy'needa Penland

All rights reserved. No part of this book may be reproduced or transmitted in any form or by any means electronic or mechanical, including photocopy, recording or any information storage and retrieval system now known or to be invented, without permission in writing from the publisher. The exception would be in the case of brief quotations embodied in the critical articles or reviews and pages where permission is specifically granted by the publisher. Any members of educational institutions wishing to photocopy part or all of the work for classroom use, or publishers who would like to obtain permission to include in an anthology, should send their inquiries to:

Adeenys Publishing,
P. O. Box 716
Dacula, GA 30019
adeenyspublishing@gmail.com

Books may be purchased in quantity and/or special sales by contacting the publisher.

Printed in the United States

Cover design by Sy'needa Penland

ISBN -10: 1-942863-03-9
ISBN -13: 978-1-942863-03-8

FIRST EDITION

This book is dedicated to the legacy and lifetime achievement of Dr. Maya Angelou, her profound wisdom and guidance has taught me "Why the Caged Bird Sings."

Content

PART I: Coming Full Circle

America, She Bares Her Shame	9
Balance	11
Beauty of Love	12
Black Skinned Man	13
Buried Souls Do Speak	14
Can America Be Cured of Her Hate?	16
Climax	18
Coming Full Circle	19
Conjoin My Heart	20
Curiosity	21
Dance in the Spirit of Love	22
Death of Mankind	23
Divine Energy	24
Earth, I Love Her	25
Eternity	26
Evening Star	27
Fertility	28
Forever Maya	29
Harmony	30
Hate is What Thine Eyes See	31
Healing of the Heart	32
Heaven and Earth	33

Hold Me	34
Honey Chile	35
Human Rights Protection	36
I Come in Peace	38
Inspire Me	40
It's Something about Mother Nature	41
Judgement Day	42
Just Mourn for Me	43
Justice	44
Key to My Heart	45
Let Me Live Another Day	46
Love is the Key	47
Lovelution	48
Loving Energy	49
Lucid Thoughts	50
Misery	51
Milky Way	52
Morality Lost	53
No More Fighting for Liberation	54
Old Glory	55
Peace Be Unto thy Earth	56
Prayer for Cleansing	57
Prince of Darkness	58
Purgatory	59
Rebirth	61
Reflections of My Black Skin	63
Resurrection	64
Revelation	65

Righteous Divinity	66
Risen	67
Sacred Temple of Life	68
Shackles – Chains – Injustice	69
Shadows of Darkness	70
Spirit Butterflies	71
Spirit of Love	73
Spirit, Mind, Body	74
So Afraid of Y'all	75
Still	76
Stone	77
The Angry Scribe	78
The Beauty of Love	79
The Essence of the Universe	80
The First and the Last	81
Time – Space – Matter	82
To Know Thyself is to Know Thyself	83
Truth	85
Unburden Your Heart	86
Unforgettable	87
Victory	89
Victory is a Comin	90
What if	91
Where Did I Find You?	92
Womb of Love	93
You Shall Weep No More	94
Your Abyss	95

PART II: Haikus

All Lives Matter	97
Awakening	97
Black Lives Matter	97
Circle of Life	98
Heart, Soul, Matter	98
Humanity	98
Moonlight	99
Paradise	99
Soul Love	99

PART III: Seeds of Wisdom

Spiritual Affirmations and Proverbs	101 – 115

♋ ♋ ♋

Coming Full Circle

America, She Bares Her Shame

Are your eyes so blind
you cannot see
the many lies told
of her history.

As time propels,
energies rebel
against untold truths
of your misery.

Wasteland.
Homeland.
It's all the same.
Paraded in her flag,
she bares her shame.

Her many stars and stripes
of blood she's shed,
loss souls long forgotten;
risen from the dead.

Their hate.
Your hate.
It's all the same!
Her soiled earth,
raped and maimed.

Graves go unmarked
as *Spirits* wander in the dark,
chasing hollow souls
to ignite their spark.

Lighting the path
through dimensions of time,
intertwined as *One Soul*
with the Heavenly Divine.

Settling old scores,
another year
once more;
feeding
the energy
of chaos
as she prepares
for war.

Boiling hot,
her core,
spewing her pain;
surviving centuries
of chaos
to remove
her stain.

Balance

As darkness
leads my path
to your guiding light,
illuminating the surface
of my waters,
our souls — touching,
yearning to become one.

Beauty of Love

Timeless beauty,
painted against
the dark veil of night.

Luminous crystals;
energies of light;
radiating my essence;
auras shine bright.

My *crystal*s;
My *diamonds*;
My *rubies* of love;

Dancing a harmonic symphony
of heaven's beauty
from above.

Black Skinned Man

Some may say
this skin I'm in
is a sin.

Yet each day
I live life
like I'm born again!

Rebirthed
to live the curse
I was born with
upon my birth.

But who Am I
but a Black
skinned man?

Buried Souls Do Speak

Does my righteousness offend you?
Some say I act too proud;
Say my voice speaks with temperament;
Say I boast and sing too loud.

Say I speak of untold truths
whose lies are buried deep;
Say through the surface of *Mother Earth*,
buried souls do speak.

Their injustices never righted;
Their graves go unmarked;
Wretched souls forever lost,
left to wander in the dark.

Lost souls long forgotten,
Their stench decayed and rotten;
Surfaced from the core of *Mother Earth*,
whose truths are long forgotten.

Receded by *her* waves,
marked in shallow graves;
Brought forth to cleanse us of hate,
what the living soul forever craves.

Go to sleep dear child,
as *we* put your souls to rest;
Cleanse and heal your children,
nourish them to do their very best.

Go to sleep dear child,
the fight is already won;
Bring forth new beginnings,
under the healing light of the Sun.

Go to sleep dear child,
as we prepare you for rebirth;

May the *Heavenly Universe*
always protect, nourish and bless
our beloved *Mother Earth*.

Can America Be Cured of Her Hate?

America,
"Can she be cured
of *her* hate
and *her* greed?!"

Sewn into
the very fabric
of *her* creed.

Her stars and stripes,
"Hailed as the
World's greatest nation."
Like all things artificial,
a mere fabrication.

Repeated lies;
Injustice;
Untold truth.
Generations lost;
Imprisoned;
Genocide of our youth.

What did you expect,
"Suppression
of our oppression?!
For our eyes to be
bond shut?!"

"To be treated
worse than slaves?
For our youth
to run amuck?"

Rebellion
of the *Spirit*
simply sets the soul free.

When the *Goddess* awakens
to protect *her* children,
it will alter the course
of history!!

Climax

The climatic flow
of your thermal heat
pulsates through my veins
like hot molten lava.
Permeating to the depths
of my core;
Soothing my soul
once more.

Coming Full Circle

Within the womb
of your cocoon
thine eyes cannot see,
the true essence
of *Divine* energy.

Changing lives;
Energies unknown;
Life's mystery.

Incarnation;
Liberation;
Reincarnation.

Transformation;
My true identity.

Conjoin My Heart

Nourish me,
    my soul;
Awaken my center,
    make me whole.
Conjoin my heart
    with the energy of love;
Reconnect my *Spirit*
    below,
In-between
    and above.

Curiosity

Magnetic,
Electric,
Hypnotizing;
Your essence.

Excites beyond
Smiles, or
Sculpted illusions;

Mesmerizing eyes,
Stunningly arousing.
Words unspoken,
Spirits intertwined;

Energies expound
Beyond life's mysteries;
Spell-bound.
Satisfy my curiosity.

Dance in the Spirit of Love

Come dance with me,
let my rhythm
envelope your soul.

Come dance with me,
let my essence
enter the depths
of your abode *(temple)*.

Come dance with me,
let my energy
ignite your *Spirit*.

Come dance with me,
let our two halves
become whole.

Death of Mankind

Oh My…
How history
continues to unfold,
baring all truths
from days of old.

Buried secrets
never die;
risen from the earth,
they tell no lie.

Time exists to only man,
his lies bear weight
for his *tales* to stand.

Once crumbled to the earth
they exist no more.
Nations stricken by death,
poverty, hate and war.

Divine Energy

Spread your essence
to my grace;
old memories I will erase.

Spread your wings
to the sky;
days of old,
no more long good-byes.

Majestic, elegant,
seductive you are,
your colors as vibrant
as the heavenly stars.

From the darkness
of your cocoon
you will always see,
the magical essence
of my *Divine* energy.

Earth, I Love Her

So vast is her beauty;
So deep are her depths;
The essence of life
in her every breath.

So sweet are her songs,
as she radiates
all day long.

Somber she sleeps,
to her oceans she weeps;
Calming her core
from her mountainous peaks.
Earth, I Love Her

Creator of all things;
Mother of all beings;
Ruler of the sky,
from the Universe she brings;

Protection,
Devotion,
Emotion and
Pain;

Healing her wombs
with her *Earthly* rains,
as she cleanse our souls
thus once again.
Earth, I Love Her

Eternity

Mirrored reflections,
    candid remarks.
Sweet orchid fragrance,
    the key to my heart.
Unlock my abyss
    as I welcome you in
To the doorway of Heaven,
    let the cleansing begin.

Evening Star

Arabic rhythms
of your oceans
excites my soul
from afar;
> Energizing
> my *Spirit*
> upon the rise
> of your
> *Evening Star.*

Death Valleys;
Crystal palaces;
Amulets of Heaven;
Illuminating all that you are.

Fertility

Along
    my fertile *Nile*
I nourish
    the soul of thee,
To bring forth
    abundant life;
Fertility.

Forever Maya
(Dedicated to the life time achievement of Maya Angelou)

There was something about your *voice*...
There was something about your *smile*...
There was something about your *grace*...
There was something about your *style*...

There was something about your *wisdom*,
as if it flowed from the deepest deltas
of the *Nile*.

Your words nourished *faith*;
Your heart gave with *compassion*;
Your memory is etched in stone;
Your teachings are *ever-lasting*.

Your voice sang songs of *freedom*;
Your cadence guided the way;
Illuminating our paths like an *Angel*,
never leading us astray.

As your legacy lives on *Forever*,
we know *Why the Caged Bird Sings*.
Hope is what you taught us;

To let
Freedom Sing...
Freedom Sing...
Freedom Sing...

Harmony

Amidst the wind,
    I soar;
  My angelic wings
     Seduced
    By your sensual delight.
        Your gentle breeze,
      Your mighty wind,
          Epic – Enchanting;
    Erotic.

Hate is What Thine Eyes See

I bear the torch of my ancestors,
my decaying soul fuels its flame.
My actions are not heroic,
I would rather die in shame.

Going down in the blaze of glory,
I shall tell my own story;
Rewriting the tales of history,
the God you seek has forsaken me.

I reap havoc around the globe,
my raging battles shall be told;
Adding a new chapter to the book of life,
together with chaos we live for strife.

Seducing your minds with lies and misery,
within the realm of our existence
your souls cannot see,
that *Peace* and *Love* is our enemy.

Healing of the Heart

Deep within the human heart
is where healing of the soul begins.
Miracles can happen at any time
if you cleanse away your sins.

Love, a four letter word
with powerful meaning,
it nourishes the soul
for *Spiritual* cleansing.

Heaven and Earth

Do you want me to tell you
that I love you,
and all that you are?

Do you want me to tell you
that I wished for you
upon the rise
of the *Evening Star*?

Sensing your essence
from a far,
we become one.

Heaven and Earth,
Feminine and *Masculine*
conjoined
under the loving light
of the *Sun*.

Hold Me

Hold me,
allow my (our) truth
to be told,
as a new *Era*
of our lives unfold.

With each turn
of the page,
the last page
erases remnants
of my (our) pain.
Built to last,
we shall sustain.

Beloved *Mother Earth,*
hold me once again.
Nourish my *Earthly* bosom,
heal away my pain.

Blunt forces of trauma
infused within
the Holy Grail
of my brain.

Insane, they call it,
'Morality lost',
information highway,
the *New Age Holocaust.*

Control-Alt-Delete,
I'm signing off.
It's the only way
to save my soul from
the *New Age Holocaust.*

Honey Chile

Honey Chile…
Honey Chile…
Come sit here
and rub *Moma's* feet
for a while.

Let *Moma* tell you
bout the days
Moma went butt wild;

Wild and free
like the burning passion
of the wind;
I wanted to soar,
I yearned to sin.

A young *Spirit* I was,
vibrant and alive;
I wanted to soar
as high as the sky.

I never thought
what growing would be;
There was so much to life
I wanted to see.

I never thought
these old feet would get tired;
I never thought
this old broad would retire.

Honey Chile…
Honey Chile…
Moma's feet has gotten tired,
sit here and rub *Moma's* feet,
Moma's gonna rest a while.

Human Rights Protection

Human Rights Protection is the preservation of **H**umanity through **U**nity, **M**aturity, **A**cceptance and forgiveness of all bad deeds from our past and proper **N**urturing of the evolution of humankind. To achieve such a higher moral standard for our society, we must learn to build stronger **R**elationships by being more **I**nvolved in all facets of life which governs humanity, including respect for *Mother Earth*. Through positive **G**oal setting and fostering a more harmonious mindset towards **H**elping others, unified as ONE human race, it will be easy to achieve. Most importantly, being **T**hankful for our blessings and promoting the *Art of Sharing* with others. Yet we must adopt and practice the idealism that we can achieve *Human Rights Protection,* beginning in our very own neighborhoods, by rebuilding a solid moral foundation in our homes, thus creating a more loving, peaceful and harmonious environment within our communities.

Proper **P**arenting is the key. Teach our children to take full **R**esponsibility for their actions and not be easily influenced by negativity. We must reinforce the importance of **O**bedience towards our elders and **T**each our children the importance of *Equality for ALL humankind,* no matter the race, gender, age or national origin. We must allow **C**ompassion back into our hearts, and foster in a more positive and loving value system by creating a more **T**ransparent and peaceful government and society. By **I**nspiring **O**ptimism for our future and practicing the *Art of Fair Negotiation*, justice, protection and unification, together as *One Human Race* we can achieve anything.

Most of all LOVE!!

Humanity
Unity
Maturity
Acceptance
Nurturing

Relationships
Involvement
Goal setting
Helping
Thankful
Sharing

Parenting
Responsibility
Obedience
Teaching
Equality
Compassion
Transparency
Inspiring
Optimism
Negotiation

I Come in Peace

For I am Woman,
hear me roar!
Upon my arrival
you will lock your doors.

My trumpets will sing
from the highest
mountain top;
I Come in Peace,
for God's children I will stop.

I'm the *Protector of Freedom*
Father God sent to Earth,
I've watch over *his* children
since their birth.

Guardian of Spirit,
Giver of Life,
Protector of the Soul;
God's First Wife.

Within their chords
lies truth of their existence;
Proof of all lies told by man,
revealing his true origin.

As *Guardians of Mother Earth*,
ashamed of his past,
that he was not the first
nor will be the last.

Every 1000 years
man has tried to erase me.
For I am *Him*,
He is *Me*,
Can't you see?!

For I am man
turned inside out,
like the bud of a flower
before it sprouts.

The truth lies
within each of my seeds,
before birth of mankind,
6 days I will bleed.

The blood is said to be
the curse of his birth,
for it is not so;
It's simply me stopping time
so I can go in reverse.

Inspire Me

Give me something;
> Penetrate the very depths
> of my soul.

Give me *Spiritual* inspiration,
> endless possibilities;
> Make our two halves – Whole.

It's Something about Mother Nature

It's something about *Mother Nature*,
as she welcomes my morning smile.
It's something about *Mother Nature*
that brings out my inner child.

It's something about *Mother Nature*,
as she nourishes my inner soul.
It's something about *Mother Nature*,
I never fear growing old.

It's something about *Mother Nature*
that remains a mystery.
It's something about *Mother Nature*
that grows inside of me.

Judgement Day

Don't judge me
by the skin I'm in,
if you say my skin is a sin.

Don't judge me
by the clothes I wear,
my heritage or my kinky hair.

Don't judge me
by the words I speak;
Would you rather
I be kind and meek?

As you come upon
your judgement day,
I shall speak truth
of all your evil ways.

I shall not judge
you for the skin you're in,
I shall speak of
your myriad sins.

I shall speak of your vicious lies.
I shall speak of your wicked guise.
I shall speak of your pretentious truth.
I shall speak of how you use *Jesus*
to excuse the wrong you do.

The *Mirror of Life* reveals *All*,
so before you seek to judge,
consider never to judge at all.

Just Mourn for Me

Don't put me on that stage!
Don't put me on that stage!
As you stare upon my page;

My page of life
is the image you'll see,
when God sat down long enough
to poise with me.

Each life lived,
Each lesson learned;

Each one of you
will soon get your turn
to poise for the page;

To be all dressed up
on the center stage;

But don't put me on that stage!
Don't put me on that stage!
Just mourn for me.

Justice

Judgement
Unilateral
Stalemate
Tyranny
Injustice
Criminal
Evil

Key to My Heart

I give you the key to my heart

as a token to show I care;

Inside you will find

many treasured gifts

beyond compare;

Cherished memories

for you and I to always share.

Let Me Live Another Day

Give me love,

Give me freedom;

   Let me live another day

   For a reason;

 No more pain,

 No more sorrow;

    Let me live another day

    To see tomorrow.

Love is the Key

Let those who have ears hear.
Let those who have eyes see.
Let those who are of righteousness *Spirit*
receive God's loving energy.

Lovelution is the solution
to bring about Peace.
Unity and harmony
is what this world needs.

We've arrived to the solution
to embrace our *Lovelution*,
not the path of revolution.
There is no confusion
to *Love*.

Can *Love* bring about positive change?
Can *Love* allow us to remain the same?
Can *Love* cleanse our tattered hearts?
Can *Love* give us a fresh start?

Is *Love* the right solution?
Is *Love* the cause of our confusion?
Do we need a revolution
to bring about *Love*?!

I don't know what your ears hear,
I don't know what your eyes see,
but what know for sure is
Love is the Key.

Lovelution

Love
Ohm
Vibration
Everything
Life
Unity
Togetherness
Infinite
One
Nature

Loving Energy

Constant, is the loving energy
that flows from the core
of our beloved *Mother Earth*.

Balancing her dimensions
as *Spirits* are re-birth,
in perfect harmony,
beating to the same drum.

One pulse;
One heartbeat;
One soul;
Dancing in rhythm
as *One*!

Lucid Thoughts

What am I searching for?
What is the secret behind the hidden door?
What if I answer my own lucid thoughts?
Will I find the answers I've been searching for?

Misery

Oh, *Protector* of many Nations,
Great Mother Earth you are to me.
What has happened to your surface?
Beneath the heavenly clouds,
Misery is what thine eyes see.

Milky Way

Kaleidoscope of *Heavens*,
Galaxies from afar,
Twin-souls colliding
within the abyss
of your luminous
Morning Star.

Morality Lost

Morality lost
is all but a "Cause"
to step out on faith,
restoring what once was.

Have we lost our *Divine* way?
When told to obey,
to *"believe in"*
what has led us astray.

Forced to obey *"rules"*
that are used as mere tools
to control our thoughts
and all that we do.

Mind control is a terrible thing,
not knowing if you're
coming or going,
yet it's all the same.

Two minds conjoined
are better than one,
working in synchronicity
with the *Universe*
to get the job done!

The *Holy Trinity*
makes our halves - *Three*,
realigning our souls with
Mother Earth's core
to restore *Peace*,
Love and *Unity*!

No More Fighting for Liberation

When the Supreme Court
delivered its verdict,
I said "Glory Hallelujah"
the LGBT community deserves it!!

No More Fighting for Liberation
for the entire LGBT nation.

As they begin
their weekend celebration,
giving praise to their nation,
let us raise a toast
to their victory.

As we join in celebration
over the entire Nation,
for their liberation;
Praise be unto thee.

Finally....
Their anguished souls
are set free!
Glory be to God
for their victory!!!

Old Glory

From far and near
yet in-between,
we've traveled a long journey
from what we've seen.

Crossing the Atlantic,
surviving *her* high tides,
giving praise to *Old Glory*
when no one died.

Many came to
stake their claim
on the treasures
of the *New World*.

Soon arrived mothers,
fathers and young
boys and girls.

Escaping poverty,
famine, torture,
slavery and disease;
only to arrive to the shores
of America's misery.

Peace Be Unto thy Earth

Oh, *Heavenly Divine* energy

I call upon thine eyes to see,

heal our pain and misery.

Fill our hearts with *Love* once more

as *Peace on Earth* is restored.

Forgive us of our daily sins

as a *New Era of Love* begins.

Prayer for Cleansing

Oh, *Divine Source of Energy*,
I call upon thine eyes to see.
Allow our efforts
and deeds to be done
under the healing light
of the *Sun*.

For in *our* names
we shall bear,
truth of *our* own despair.
We shall pay for All *our* sins
as *our* new lives begin;
Forever cleanse us of *our* sins.

Prince of Darkness

I surrender my fears to *Darkness*,
my soul blinded to his misery.
Hate is his companion,
God's light he does not see.

He nourishes fruit
that's unforgiven,
he preys on the living
and prepares a feast
for his thanksgiving.

Darkness bears fruit
in his garden of sin,
as he seeks to possess your soul
each time new life *(thoughts)* begins.

Purgatory

Release me from your womb,
let thine eyes see the light.
For score, centuries ago,
my soul was taken in the night.

I've bore the fate of my ancestors,
the proud *Mandingo* man,
who was chained and kidnapped
from his native land.

Held captive, left to die,
Pain, suffering and misery
became his way of life.

Forced to lie in shackles,
battling deadly waves,
to be cradled in her bosom,
Mother Africa he surely craved.

Until my return
I shall shed no tear,
within my heart and soul
Mother Africa I hold you near.

Arriving to the West,
I was forced to do my best.
I've built bridges and railroads
as I proudly beat my chest.

I've survived bondage and chains,
acres of sugar cane,
cotton fields
and molten tar pits,
yet that fatal ditch
is what I did not see,
all these centuries years
my God survived me.

To my Irish and Scottish brothers,
those forced to say goodbye
to their mothers
for promises of riches,
to be taken from the indigenous.

Sadly to their arrival
they ached for survival
and many missed the boat;
the untamable land
was far from a joke.

Forced to mine the caves;
Forced to break through mountains,
to make way for a canal
or segregated water fountain.

Not familiar with their cause,
the indigenous were forced to give up
what they loved the most,
to adhere to manmade laws.

Forced on reservations,
a modern day plantation;
Forced into submission,
to abandon their mission
which was to protect *Mother Earth*
from *Alien* invasion.

Rebirth

Loving *souls* you are to me;
Rebirthed from different realms
through synchronicity.

Recycled through
dimensions of time;
Living *Spirits* – intertwined.

Universally connected
to the same chord of life,
Mother Earth's core;
The first seed life.

Her healing waters
which soothes her core,
shall come forth to cleanse
our souls once more.

As we celebrate
the season of *Spring;*
New life – Rebirth souls
she'll bring.

Brought forth to guide us
towards her healing light;
Protecting our souls
as we sleep at night.

Awakening our *Spirits*
to *God's Morning Glory*,
Amen Ra's Sunlight.

As she sits to the *East*
of the *West* below;
New seeds she shall bestow.

To cleanse her sons of hate;
A better life for his wives,
sons and daughters
he will soon create.

To teach them the difference
between right and wrong;
To teach them obedience,
how to get along.

To become proud protectors
of her sacred land;
To grow stronger and wiser
to better understand;

The true nature and ways
of our *Heavenly Divine,
Great Mother Earth*,
as she welcomes us all
to our *Spirits'* rebirth.

Reflections of My Black Skin

"My Black is Beautiful"
are the words that
resonate from my
flawless *Black Skin*.

"My Black Don't Crack!"
Are my thoughts
when I by-pass the isles
of endless beauty products,
advertising *"age-defying"* beauty?

I never have to worry about
being traded in for a
younger version of my-self
because I look younger
than I did 20 years ago.

I love the younger
version of me!
Because I've *Saged*
into my *Natural Black Beauty*.

"Fountain of Youth is more like it!"
When *God* designed the *Black Woman*
in *her* image, *She* broke the mold!

Resurrection

Each step I traveled
along your desert *Nile*,
feet worn, heart stricken;
Dry sands - oozes bile.

Devastation;
Castration;
Annihilation!

Anguished souls
resurrected
to nourish
the souls of thee;

Brought forth
in the name of *Love*,
to cleanse thy *Earth*
of hate and misery.

Revelation

History,
A collection of *truths*;
Someone else' lies.

Blind to evil doers
who suffer
their own demise.

Insecurities of the soul
ferments through to the skin;
Flesh covered with fallacies
of man's original sin.

Righteous Divinity

A dedication
to those that have fallen;
Your heroic sacrifice
was your calling.

When *God* of all *Gods*
raises the dead,
the fallen heroes
will break *her* bread.

Many are chosen,
few will endure
what the *Divine Goddess*
has in store. Once few,
many more.

Earthly souls
have grown to plenty,
brought forth
to cleanse thy Earth
by *Righteous Divinity*.

Risen

Buried kingdoms
    long forgotten;
Crystal palaces
    ordained in gold.
Stolen treasures,
    behold;
Resurrection,
    incarnation;
Broken spells,
    Armageddon.

Sacred Temple of Life

Desert canvas,
oasis of life.
    Gatekeeper of Heaven,
    man's first wife.

Timeless crystals
beneath my feet;
    Heaven's oasis,
        buried deep.

Shackles — Chains — Injustice

Shackles,
Chains,
Injustice.

Chains,
Injustice,
Shackles.

Injustice,
Shackles,
Chains.

No matter the order
It's all the same.

Shadows of Darkness

Energies released,
sources unknown;
Drawn to *Spirit*,
forever will roam.

Seekers of light,
invaders of homes;
A quest for freedom,
destination unknown.

Shadows of Darkness,
purveyors of truth;
Particles of matter,
reflecting all that we do.

Spirit Butterflies

Spirit Butterflies,
Spirit Butterflies,
rescue me from pain.
Deliver me from darkness,
my hollow life of shame.

This cocoon of life,
a living hell;
Where misery
is my companion;
Where dead energy
loves to dwell.

In darkness I scream
as my life is turned inside out;
As my last breathe fades away,
I can no longer shout.

Time – Still
Life – Motionless
Space – No more

No air to breath;
No room to move;
My *Spirit* yearns
for all of you.

Nourish my soul
with the *Essence of Life;*
Cleanse my *Spirit*
of misery, as well as
human strife.

Nourish me,
upon this tiny leaf;
Nourish my soul
with your *Essence,*
rooted from your *Ancient Tree.*

Nourish me;
My center;
My birth place of life;
Rejuvenate my *Essence*
with the *Energy of Life*.

Life once lived,
Spirit reborn –
Transformed
under the healing light
of the *Sun*.

Spirit Butterflies,
as I spread my wings
to the sky,
I bid farewell
to my old life;
May your loving energy
never die.

Spirit of Love

Oh, *Great Spirit* above
whose heart thine eyes does not see;
Open our hearts and souls
to welcome your ecstasy.

Rain down the *Spirit of Love*
from the vast heavens above;
Fill our earthly vessels
with your *Great Spirit of Love*.

Let not hate exist within,
forgive us of our daily sins;
Cleanse thy earth thus once again.

May the mountains rise
above my tides;
May your hearts be pure
thus forever more;
Peace and Love
I will restore.

May your souls be blessed,
you have passed the test;
May your souls be cleansed
and DO NOT sin again!

Spirit, Mind, Body

Spirit,
Mind,
Body,
One.

The soul
dancing
in unison
with the *Sun*.

Energies
of emotions,
Fusion of Love;

Enveloping
all *Below*,
In-between
and *Above*.

So Afraid of Y'all

Lives are never lost
without a reason.
To shoot a black man
in America
is open season.

So much hate
for a black man's soul
can make a gun-toting fool
feel bold.

Pow! Pow! Pow!

Lights out nigger,
as I slowly pull the trigger,
"This is for my Pappy!"

Pow! Pow! Pow!

Lights out nigger,
as I slowly pull the trigger,
"This is for my Pa!"

Pow! Pow! Pow!

Lights out nigger,
as I slowly pull the trigger,
"This is for my insanity!"
Cause I'm so afraid of Y'all.

Still

As I sit here in thought,
energies pulsating
in rhythmic vibration
with the heart and soul
of our beloved *Mother Earth,*
I become one with *her Divine Spirit,*
as she prepares me for re-birth.

I've written poetry
about *her* vast beauty,
her soothing sounds,
her melodic energies,
as *she* flows in synchronicity
with the *Universe,*
pulsating up and down.

Flowing – *her* energies,
vibrating to *One* pulse,
One rhythm – *One* sound;
Still…
Pulsating up and down.

Like the sound of nothing.
Yes, nothing.
You can't hear *her,*
feel *her* pulse,
become *One* with *her* rhythm.
Let *her* rhythmic vibrations
flow through you,
become *One* with you.

Still…
Is *her* movement.
She doesn't travel all around.
Still…
Is her movement,
as she pulsates up and down.
Still…

Stone

You brought clarity
to my life,
balancing my *Spirit;*
no more strife.

You ground me
with your essence,
your magnificent glory;
like all precious gems,
your essence tells a story.

As mystic as the seas,
you shine as bright as
the *Heavenly* skies;
radiating *God's Glory*,
a true reflection of life.

The Angry Scribe

"I've seen so much
since I've been alive,"
wrote the words of
The Angry Scribe.

I'm not sure
just where to begin;
I've born witness to
so much sin;

As history
repeats itself,
again and again.

As I prepare my message
to the *Most High*,
bearing witness
to the source of man's pain;

I dare not
report false truths,
to disguise the evil nature
of man's shame.

Pondering back and forth
to debate his choice
became too much
for the *Scribe* to bear;

Putting down his pen,
taking one last breath,
he needed historical notes
to compare.

The Beauty of Love

Encapsulate my heart
with your *Spirit* of ecstasy;
Illuminate my flesh,
allow my soul to see;

Your shining light,
a nucleus of
Universal Love;
My daylight
shining star;

Oh, how I yearn to feel
the beauty of your *Love*
from galaxies from afar.

The Essence of the Universe

Binaural beats;

Synchronistic rhythms;

Pulsating sounds;

Vibrational energies

The Essence of the Universe, all around.

The First and the Last

Have we not come
to actualize
the depths of our pain?

Capsulize the source
of its existence,
it's *all the same*!

Hundreds of years,
trapped in purgatory,
forced to accept the many lies
of *His'* story.

Unspoken *truths*
speaks from hell;
Demons trapped
between dimensions;
Only time will tell...

Anguished souls
left to perish
did not die;
Risen above for cleansing,
to erase away the lies!!

Who is God?
Dare you now ask...
For I am the *ONE*,
The First and the Last!

Time – Space – Matter

As I inhale thee,
I become *One*
with thee.

Energies felt;
Rhythmic vibrations
pulsates through
to my *soul* – my *core*.

Time…
Space…
Matter…

One rhythm,
One movement,
One pulse,
One heartbeat;

Vibrating
in perfect harmony
with the heart and soul
of our beloved
Mother Earth.

To Know Thyself is to Know Thyself

For total and complete liberation
of the *Black Man's Soul*;

Will require him to erase
all the lies he's been told;

Will require him to believe that
he has the heart of a lion;

Will require him to believe
that his soul isn't dying;

Will require him to believe in
all things created by *God*;

Will require him to break free of
the shackles and the rod;

Will require him to know that
deep within his heart and soul
is a breast plate made of *Gold*;

Will require him to imagine himself
along the *Ivory Coast of the Nile*;

Will require him to know that
his seeds are the most fertile;

Will require him to accept
his true faith and inheritance;

Will require him to know that
the *Universal God* is his deliverance;

Will require him to cleanse thy *Spirit*
and set thy soul free;

Will require him to know that the flesh
is what harbors his pain and misery.

Truth

As I continue to stand
on the side of righteousness,
Truth bears my name.

My origins have been passed down
in your history books,
they say *God* is my name.

I've watched the destruction of
Mother Earth from afar,
I'm *her* honing beacon
called a *Star*;

Forever calibrating *her* axis,
keeping *her Spirit* aligned
with your souls,
reinforcing it each day,
as human evolution (history) unfolds.

Man's addiction to chaos
has spread to the core of
our beloved *Mother Earth*;
May *Peace and Love* be restored
as *she* prepares you for rebirth.

Unburden Your Heart

Anguished *souls*,
your weary *Spirits*
cannot rest;
Burdened by
the angry beast,
your hearts and souls
it shall bequest.

Unforgettable

Another year has come and gone,
as I pay my respect
to those we mourn,
as recent as twice yesterday.

When I read the caption,
"*Natalie Cole* has died,"
tears began to well in my eyes;

Unforgettable was the thought
that came to me.
Angelic was her voice
as she sang with
grace, beauty and dignity.

Another headline that came to soon,
Bill Cosby is still in the news?!
What the hell is really going on?!
As I struggle to focus to write this poem.

Why should this phase me?
Why should I get caught up in his misery?
But as a veteran of the stage – not even his old age
can save him now, as he surrenders his throne
to take a bow.

What has become of this country I call home?
America the Beautiful, where I was originally born.
Now I look around at many strangers,
foreigners from lands I've seen,
settling in America to escape their pain and misery.

As we enter into the year 2016,
I shall reflect on all I've seen;
Embarking on a new journey
to scribe a sequel to my own story.

Coming Full Circle, a poem I once wrote,
scribing the energy of words
my father's *Spirit* spoke;
As if knowing what words would be spoken,
when we bid him farewell he left a token.

Blessing me with mystic gifts
to fill my treasure chest;
His *Spirit* watches over me
to ensure I'll do my very best.

Unforgettable, Father is what you are to me;
Please join hands with the *Elders*
as they welcome home, Natalie.

Victory

Under the shadow
of your moonlit veil,
I dwell;

Forced to live
my life in hell.
Upon birth,
cursed into sin;

Rebirthed;
Revolving;
No beginning;
No end.

Awakened,
my eyes see
reality.

No veil;
No hell;
As my *Spirit*
exhale;

Light,
Glory,
Victory!

Victory is a Comin

At last,
At last,
Victory is a Comin.

At last,
At last,
Victory is a Comin.

I hear the triumphs singing
praise of *Victory*.
Singing *Glory Hallelujah*,
my *God* has rescued me.

My soul held captive
in the abyss of your hell;
A place where *demons*
and *fallen angels*
prefer to dwell;

Battling years
of deep oppression,
my soul has arisen;
escaping captivity
in your prison.

Rising to the *Zenith*
of the horizon,
I have the courage
of a *Lion*.

At last,
At last,
Victory is a Comin.

At last,
At last,
Victory is a Comin.

What if

What if we could achieve a *World of Peace*,
and always be kind to those we meet,
to a stranger we meet on the street.

A stranger of a different "kind",
welcomed by the *Spirit of Love*,
Love is blind.

Love exists within all living things
that intertwines the souls
of all human beings.

We are not strangers to one another,
the *loving* energy of our souls
are connected to our *Great Mother*,

Our beloved *Mother Earth*
who *loves* us all the same.
Let us achieve a *World of Peace*
in the *Spirit* of *her Holy Name*.

Where Did I Find You?

Where did I find you,
from the *Angels* above?
You were dispersed from *heaven*
with abundant energy of *Love*.

You speak words
of ancient wisdom,
the *Bearer of Truth*,
recalibrating my soul
to the days of my youth.

Your luminous *Spirit*
crosses all dimensions
of *Father-Time*.
Twin souls,
One soul;
Intertwined.

Womb of Love

I bore the seeds of mankind
yet his eyes are too blind to see,
"Why, after all these centuries
my wrath survived thee?!"

Protector of his soul,
my wrath is surely bold
yet the truth of my existence
remains a mystery.

Close your eyes dear child,
let your senses draw me near.
For it is not my wrath
your wretched souls should fear.

For I gave you breathe
when I delivered you into my light,
protected within my *Womb of Love*,
my energy gives you sight.

Trapped within the *Womb of Hate*,
you seek to destroy what I create.
As if birthing new seeds
will erase away my history,
yet I remain a mystery?!

As I reconnect my *Spirit*
to mend your broken hearts;
May the energy of *hate*
never again tear us apart.

You Shall Weep No More

Oh, *Heavenly Divine Universe*
pour down your healing rain;
Cleanse the surface of thy Earth,
remove *her* evil stains.

Oh, my beloved *Mother Earth*
you shall weep no more;
From the depths
of your ocean floor
I shall rise once more,
to heal you from your core;
You shall weep no more.

Your Abyss

As I lay here
beside you,
ready to extend myself
inside you;

I yearn to enter
your moist,
welcoming abyss.

I'm excited
by your touch,
your wetness,
your breathe;

Your sweetness,
beckons me to explore
your intimate depths.

You welcome me
with pure pleasure,
such warm delight.

To the very depths
of your soul,
I'm sure to ignite.

Haikus

All Lives Matter

Peace, Love, Unity;
One collective human race;
Compassion for all.

Awakening

Breath beyond *Spirit*,
Energies beyond this realm;
Eroticism.

Black Lives Matter

Is brutality
My fate? My reality?
My life's destiny?

Circle of Life

Oceans, Motions, Turns;
Evolution, Life's patterns;
Humanity – One.

Heart, Soul, Matter

Beating to one pulse;
Multidimensional realms;
All void in between.

Humanity

Life preserved. One race;
Compassion, Respect for all;
Love beyond measure.

Moonlight

The light of darkness,
Symphony of God's Glory;
Crystal explosion.

Paradise

Heaven's *Oasis*,
Fruit of the Earth awakened.
The abyss of life.

Soul Love

Essence of your love
Envelopes the Universe.
Soul Love, Our Love, One.

Seeds of Wisdom

♋ ♋ ♋

"*Truth* is what grounds you to source energy."

"*Truth* beyond measure is nothing to measure because its origin is *truth.*"

"*Truth* is what the blind eye sees, because *truth* is blind."

"If the punishment fits the crime, then let it be *truth.*"

"There is nothing to fear but *truth.*"

"*Truth* will lead you to discover that you've been living in *truth* your entire life."

♋ ♋ ♋

♋ ♋ ♋

"Once the veil has been lifted, *truth* will welcome you with a smile."

"Being honest and *truthful* is the joy of righteousness."

"Compassion will lead you on a journey of *truth*, welcome the adventure."

"*Truth* shall shield you from the light, t*ruth* lives in darkness."

"Lies will weaken a man's soul to decay, long before he can truly experience the joys of life."

"*Trust, loyalty* and *integrity* is what life has taught me thus far. In the end, I trust in only *God* as my true friend."

♋ ♋ ♋

♋ ♋ ♋

"If the world was built in a day, that's a lie."

"If history told the *truth*, it will expose all its lies."

"The mastery of telling a lie is to always know the difference between it and the *truth*."

"To live without a lie means you've never lived at all."

"If a lie exposes the good in all things, then let it be good."

"Lies will go on forever until you seek to know the *truth*."

≋ ≋ ≋

"If *truth* is a lie, then let all lies be *truth*."

"Lies are the building blocks of *truth*, for it is *truth's* foundation."

"Life is nothing but a script, eventually everyone will get their turn on the *Great Stage of Life*."

"Nourish your soul with the *Essence of Life*, for it contains the seedlings of *love* and *joy*."

"An empty soul is vulnerable to lies; keep it filled with *truth*."

"You are a child of *God* and *God's* DNA is within you. If you believe in the power that you were born with; the true *God* will run religion out of business."

♋ ♋ ♋

"Never allow your *Spirit* to fall captive to silence."

"Buried deep within the human soul is *Peace*, let's honor and respect *her*, *she* deserves our *love* and *protection*."

"Life is to be adored, embraced, loved and most of all lived."

"What goes up, naturally cycles around before returning to the ground, so make sure your thoughts are always loving."

"*Love* puts you in harmony with all Universal beings."

"Whisper softly to *God*, *she's* always listening."

♋ ♋ ♋

♋ ♋ ♋

"*Universal Love* is the antidote that will permanently heal our *souls* of hate."

"When *God* created *love, she* created the cure to heal all *Spiritual* ailments."

"Hate only needs the energy of hate to fuel itself yet *love* requires the energy of *God (Mother Earth)* to purify the human soul. The energy of *God* is always in control."

"To break a man's *Spirit* gives you free access to his soul."

"Take time to listen to the sounds of *Nature, she's* always listening."

"Beloved *Mother Earth*, creates all, nourishes all and heals all living beings."

♋ ♋ ♋

♋ ♋ ♋

"Lovely is the sound of *nature* on a brisk summer morning."

"The cheerful sound of singing birds speaks of a world we all share."

"Morning *Sun*, noonday rain, lends to a restful summer night."

"Words carry vibrations that both soothes and stimulates the heart, fine-tune your emotions before you speak."

"The soul of a man is guided by his moral character, for it should never be misguided by other *Spirits*."

"Those that serve you are simply learning to become the master of your soul."

♋ ♋ ♋

"Once - twice, bitten by temptation that fuels the flame of the burning soul."

"Sweetness, bitterness, it's all the same; leaving your *Spirit* craving for the other."

"*Dark – Light*; shadowed colors of *Love*; dancing a harmonic symphony against the veil of the *Universe*."

"Words transmit rhythmic vibrations to the *Universe*; kind words are always soothing to her soul."

'Love, joy, laughter and praise; gives honor to the *Glory of God*.

"When you are practicing someone else's belief system, you are not practicing that of your own."

♋ ♋ ♋

"Faith is the root word of faithful, to live a faithful life you must have faith."

"Every thought has a seed, if you are not prepared to nourish it, be careful what thoughts you plant in a person's mind."

"The heart is blind to kindness, when you are kind to someone, you open their eyes to see the loving light inside of you."

"As you soar above the earth, spread you wings."

"Life is a dance. If you follow the rhythm of your soul you will never be out of step."

"You can never stop learning, when you do, you begin dying."

♋ ♋ ♋

"Allow *Mother Earth* to nourish your mind, by being 'open-minded' to *(receive)* experience her *Essence*, which has evolved mankind."

"Allow your thoughts to explore new realities that only you and the *Universe* can see."

"Home is where happiness, love and laughter begins. May your home always be filled with blessings."

"When you seek advice beyond *Self*, you open a doorway to your soul."

"A road less traveled is a journey most treasured."

"In the *Game of Life* there is always a beginning and end, everything in between is left up to you and *God* to negotiate."

♋ ♋ ♋

"No ladder is too high to climb when you step outside the vortex of your mind."

"By taking the path less traveled will allow your mind to venture beyond the unknown. Let your *Spirit* be your guide."

"Time - Space - Matter are all *One*, under the illuminating light of the Sun."

"*Love* is more than giving and receiving, true *love* is about believing in *love*."

"Before you seek advice from man, first seek advice from God, by simply asking, "Is it OK to follow the advice of man?""

"Destiny is a destination traveled, before you know where you're headed."

♋ ♋ ♋

♋ ♋ ♋

"Know where you're going before following some else's lead."

"Don't fall victim to another man's ego."

"There is only one true master of the *Universe*, for the master created both the heavens and the earth."

"Always follow your first instinct, when you do, you'll be following in the footsteps of your *Spirit Guides.*"

"Unless you've been there before, how can you give someone advice on where they are going?"

"Like the core of the earth, the human heart is protected by many layers."

♋ ♋ ♋

♋ ♋ ♋

"Only the gatekeeper holds the key to unlock the door to the human heart, keep it guarded at all times."

"Your home is your sanctuary, guard and protect it at all cost."

"The human heart is the *Protector of the Soul*, guard it with your life."

"*Love* is a 4 letter word with multiple meanings. A person's actions will convey how they construe their definition of *Love*."

"When you evolve to *Love*, you have *evolved*."

"How can you teach someone which path to follow in in life, for only *Spirit Guides* knows the best path for the human soul."

♋ ♋ ♋

♋ ♋ ♋

"Don't be fooled by a fool. And don't play the fool for another man's folly."

"Guidance beyond *Self* is a lesson learned."

"In the *Game of Life* there are many rules, always know what cards you hold and which ones you need before you draw a new one from the deck."

"In the *Game of Life*, don't play too many cards to soon. Keep your *eyes* on your opponent and always keep your *Ace in the Hold*."

"Never show all your cards to your opponent because you'll never know their final move."

"Never *showoff* all your moves to your opponent; their ultimate goal is to become the master of your game."

♋ ♋ ♋

"You can't teach an old dog new tricks, leave it up to *Mother Nature*."

"Before you embark on a new challenge in life, ground your *Spirit* with the *Soul of the Universe* and be prepared for an incredible journey."

"Spread *Joy, Peace, Unity* and *Love* by always giving honor to our beloved *Mother Earth*."

"Glory be to the *Most High, Below* and *In-between*!"

"*Spirituality* is a lifestyle, it's not a religion."

"*Love* is the power of living. Start living."

♋ ♋ ♋

Dedicated to the Power of Love

www.ingramcontent.com/pod-product-compliance
Lightning Source LLC
Chambersburg PA
CBHW070052120426
42742CB00048B/2480